Death Club

By

John F. Green

First published by AuthorHouse 04/14/04

ISBN: 1-4140-8267-3 (e-book)
ISBN: 1-4184-3624-0 (Paperback)

Library of Congress Control Number: 2004091762

This book is printed on acid free paper.

Printed in the United States of America
Bloomington, IN

The idea of a survival guide to terminal illness may seem like an oxymoron; and in fact it is. The reality is that if you die you haven't survived at all. So what is this book about? What is the purpose?

If you have a terminal illness you will soon understand that it is not nearly as romantic and glamorous as it is portrayed in the movies. The truth is, that it is a painful, grief filled, horrendous experience that will test the fiber of your being and define your truths in a light that you have never seen. What does that mean? What truths? Don't be so cryptic you may think; and you are right.

Let us begin with the most obvious and rudimentary aspect of this book. What is terminal illness? It is many diseases that we see around us every day like MS, CP, Cancer, AIDS, Parkinson's, Lupus, Rheumatoid Arthritis, Diabetes. It is any of the many strange and debilitating diseases that somehow leave us physically altered and hasten us to death whether it is a month or twenty years. For the purposes of this book the focus will be on Cancer and AIDS and others that create an urgency for reformation due to their swift and fatal speed.

The process of these diseases ebbs and flows. There will be times when you will be able to manage your symptoms with medication and alternative therapies, and then you will have periods of no control. This is the simple truth of this process; there is nothing we can do to change this. Don't think for a minute that this is a powerless place to be. This book is about empowering you to manage and fight your disease. Recognizing when to fight and when to lie down (on the sofa) is the most difficult part of this experience.

There will be moments when you want to throw in the towel and just die but it isn't so easy. Having thought about dying a lot in the past thirteen years I have realized that it just doesn't happen that fast. I always think to myself that if I die then it wins!

I have been fighting AIDS for thirteen years and have had some very real and painful setbacks. Somehow I manage to bounce back each time and regroup; but not without compromises and losses. These evil monsters bring us along for a while and then slam us to the mat when we are least prepared. We will be humbled again and again. When we think we are improving something as simple as our most recent blood work will prove us wrong.

I am sorry that the information in this book may come to late for some people. Some of us in the death club get a diagnosis and before we have a chance to respond we are gone. That sounds so grim but there are times when I think a quick death would be kinder. Soldiering along for endless years wears at the core of your soul and forces you to become more resourceful and resilient than the year before. Are we talking about futility? Not at all. I will repeat over and over; if we die then it wins.

We of the death club exist in an altered awareness, a heightened state of being. Sometimes we are blind and then we can see through walls into caves quite dark with confusion and stupidity. We receive a sense of the shear value of life.

The enigmatic resonance of a clap of thunder or the squeal of a child in a playground. We learn the difference between truth and a very gentle lie. We understand the sheer glory of a clean, crisp sheet or a single white candle. There is a truth we come to know, an innocence we recapture, and a clarity of existence and courage of great warriors.

In the course of writing this book I will be traveling with you through the years I have spent researching and learning how to fight. I will try to let you know what to expect and hopefully make your journey a little less painful. I love you all and want you to know you are not alone.

FEAR

We all know the expression "There is nothing to fear but fear itself"; how true. It is completely acceptable and most likely guaranteed that at some point you will feel afraid while combating terminal illness. If you don't; you are superhuman.

Being afraid of death itself is the first and ongoing obstacle. We all fear death at some point in our lives. Some people combat that fear by developing their spiritual beliefs and asking the answers to all of those mysterious questions that pervade the existence of even the simplest minded beings. Who am I? Where do I fit in? Will I get into heaven? Is there Heaven? You know the drill. Good luck. We can only

John F. Green

hope to come to some peace with these questions because we really have to die to get the answers. Hope.

The real fear is the fear of pain. Many people will say I don't care how I go I just don't want to die painfully. With TI (terminal illness) there will be pain. It is your job to let your care providers know when it comes so they can help you manage it. Please do not bare pain you don't need to bare. This will dull you to other things and make you edgy and crabby. Who needs that? I believe it is better to be a little detached from the pain meds than completely hostile because of the pain. You will need to keep your wits so that you can think things through and make decisions about your life.

Pain is not a permanent situation. It will come and go. There will be times when you won't have any and others when you will manage it very well. Sometimes it will be out of control and you will have to cry out for help.

There are other fears. Fear of rejection, financial and career things, decision and worry fear, fear of loneliness. The list of fears is endless. You will discover your own. The main thing to keep in mind is that when you are in a fearful place to speak out. Tell someone or everyone "I am afraid"; "Help me work through this fear". Sometimes just airing your fear helps because those that love you may feel the same way and then it can be diffused.

The biggest part of self-empowerment is taking the power away from your fears. When I have discussed my fears with my mother and father I often feel them getting uncomfortable but then we talk it out and they usually are in the same place with me. The best part of those talks is when we all get it out and have a nervous laugh of relief. It bonds you.

Be warned that you will have nights laying awake and processing your fear of a medical procedure or treatment that is coming the next day. The best way to kill this fear is to talk to your doctor ahead of time and learn everything you can to relax your fears and again take the power out of it. I get stressed sometimes just knowing I have to have blood labs. Lets face it; no one wants to have pain or discomfort in the course of medical testing. The violation of invasive testing is just plain awful. It is. I hate it.

LOVE

In the Death Club love is the all encompassing and most valuable resource. It is the total of all things that come and go, exist and disappear. Love will see you through any obstacle and give you reason to exist when all other reasons elude you. It will be found in the tiniest leaf and the biggest sky.

To survive you will have to map out all the love in your life and solidify it like you never have before. Any love that is weak or half- hearted has be locked down or dumped like rotten peaches. The loves that are strong should be fortified with communication and trust.

Who can you depend on? Who loves you unconditionally? Who is in it for the long haul? Learn the names and keep the list close at hand. The journey in a Death Club GT with cruise out of control is not an easy one. You need to know who has the spare tires and who can charge the battery. You will be surprised at the people that will come from nowhere with more unconditional love than you can imagine. They will surface and shower you with compassion and tenderness and generosities of time and sometimes money. You will be humbled by them and love them so dearly that your heart will break.

Some will leave you cold, as they run in fear and fail to be able to face the idea of losing you. Some will not have the skills to know how to help you and so they will shy away. Some will simply be fearful of sharing your space due to some internalized phobia about death, contagiousness or God knows what. Let them go and don't judge them.

There is also a category of people who love you so well that the shear thought of losing you is more than they can comprehend. They would be so lost or diminished that they cannot conceive the loss. Try to be most kind to these people. A life long friend may suddenly seem to be freezing you out and the truth is their fear of loss is clutching them in a state of terror. I had a friend like this share with another friend that they based so much of their identity on my love and support and model of life to them that losing me was an insurmountable fear. When I discovered this how was I to feel but honored? Had I not found this out I would have thought they didn't care enough to be with me. They wanted to but couldn't handle the fear and pain on their part. I love that friend more dearly than ever. I am blessed by them.

Many of us have spouses or life partners that are with us every day. If we do not solidify this primary relationship it will become very fragile. I'm not big on exercises but if you can make a written list for this person defining everything that they mean to you, why you depend on them, the value you place on the relationship, and just how much you love them; it will be invaluable. Present them with this list. Put it on the refrigerator. Keep it by the bed. You may be too

John F. Green

tired or weak to tell them later. They may be exhausted with care giving. They may be grief stricken. All you have to say is "Darling, you are everything on the list and more to me today, thank you." It will mean more to them than you know. It is multi dimensional. Protect and nurture this primary relationship. Defend it to anyone who judges it. In sickness and in health.

Outsiders may judge your caregiver but you know who held you while you puked at three AM and who went to the Seven-Eleven at two AM to get a bottle of ginger ale so you could get something in your body. You know who took care of the dog and put the kids to bed. You know who looks at you with knowing and unrestrained tenderness, and fear and still manages to stay by your side. Cleanse your house with this person at the beginning and set the stage for the toughest pile of shit you'll ever wade through.

NEW LOVE

What? How can this be? I'm going to shit and you're in love with me. It may seem impossible that a new love could develop while you are dieing but I don't think this is so uncommon.

If you think about the big picture the whole thing makes a lot of sense. You are having all of these changes in your life. You metamorphosis into a whole new being. You understand and see the universe in a new light. You know some of the great secrets of life and begin practicing a new religion of self- understanding. For the first time in your life you hear birds and tides and the crust of the earth shifting a million miles away.

You may be weak, skinny or tired. You may be bald from chemotherapy or pale from malnutrition. Then for some reason you have a glow of enlightenment from the heavens above and the Earth worms below and presto. You are a being of beauty and purity. You are "singing electric" as the poet says.

The attraction of this is astounding. You may not think anyone would be attracted to you but other beings of your resonance will see you and find you beautiful. I saw a woman with a bald- head and puffiness from radiation at the clinic one day and all I could think was how grand she looked. Her truth was on display and she was radiant. I smiled to her in the way we Death Clubbies smile to each other. She read my mind and smiled back. She read my mind.

You may think that someone who suddenly shows an interest in you is really just needing to fill some care-giving martyr roll and this may be very real. You would be well advised to be cautious. It is possible however that their affection is real. I have had more relationships in the years I have had

Aids than before. I also have had Aids for nearly a third of my life. Holy Hell! What a realization. My experience has been that only one of those people seemed to have some nobility problem. The rest just thought I was a good guy and wanted to fall in love with me. It can happen. It can be wonderful. I was at the end of a relationship when I became HIV positive. I didn't think I would find love again. I did. It was a great gift. I will find it again. I'm not afraid to be loved any more. Love me, I may be fighting for my life but I'll include you in it anyway. Don't be so leery of it that you cheat yourself of joyfulness and belonging. Love, love, love. It will heal you.

TRUTH

My motto for life is:

Speak the truth,

Know what is real.

Be proud of who you are.

With that said, what is the truth? My truth is that I will not accept defeat to the disease that is in my body without a sincere and arduous fight. I will not allow myself to be treated as less than whole. I will not hide behind fear or self- pity when I can be seeking information to conquer my disease. I will love as hard as I ever have and play even harder.

Truth is the difference between being armed and walking in the dark. If your doctor does not tell you the whole truth you are defenseless to that which is withheld. If you are not in truth to your doctor than you cannot fault a lack of action to find resolve with a symptom. You lie, you die! Harsh I know but I am telling you the truth.

Be in truth to the people you love. It is their right as much as yours to know where you stand and where they stand in retrospect. I'm not saying you should tell your sister that her new hair color is wrong, although noble a thing to do, but tell her you are afraid and you need her hand to hold. Tell her you are too sick to come to her birthday party and that you will see her privately at a later date. Tell her you really can't afford a gift because you had to pay some out of pocket medical expenses and then, what you would give her if you were rich. Tell her you love her for being your sister and that she is a precious gift to you every day of your life. Tell her you were glad she defended you against that bigger kid on the bus. Tell her all the truths of your life and she will know you at last.

Be in truth with your friends. Don't let confusion, fear and hurt drive people away. Speak your truth to them. Love them. I can't say this enough, love them all.

Being a person of truth brings so much to the table. I tell people if I dream about them good or bad. I share concerns for their lives. I tell them about instinctive feelings I have and perceptions of them that to me seem visible. I have just become this truthful little pain in the ass. For some reason they all seem to love me for it. It allows all of us to look at the bullshit in our lives and bust it up and haul it out for good. It allows us to work out karma and fix crap from prior lives together to cleanse our souls in a very real way.

Most importantly, remember that truth is individual. My truth and yours may vary a great deal on the same topic or experience. Your truth may be that your father was an alcoholic and mine was clearly not. You may see that your perception is your truth and someone as close as your spouse may have a different view. That is completely acceptable.

Find your version of the truth and own it the best you can and be prepared to clarify it if asked and you want to.

Most of all live the truth. I honor the people who have been truthful to me no matter what the price; more than I honor the nicest liar. When you are dying what good is a liar? When you think you have to lie, also think if you will get the chance to explain it later; or if you should just save valuable time and come out with the truth. Be a person of truth. Your example will grow many flowers. Flowers that will bloom long after you are gone. Last thought on this for now: It gets easier as you learn how to be tactful and gentle.

VEGTABLES

You may wonder how I can talk about love and truth and include vegetables in their company. Nothing is more about love and truth than vegetables. I love them. They are life. Some of my fondest childhood memories are of staying with my mothers' parents in the country and helping with the garden. My grandfather would take me in to the garden and teach me to hoe and pull weeds. In those days his garden was organic because he didn't waste money on pesticides and chemical fertilizers. I remember him sitting me on a bench next to him and presenting me with a tomato and a salt- shaker he kept in his pocket. It tasted like the earth and sunshine. The juice ran down my arm. It was perfect. My grandmother would perch me on the edge of a small block basin behind her kitchen and with my feet in few inches of

16

well water I would shell peas or snap beans by the bushel. My little hands would do their work to earn my keep.

Vegetables will become a dear ally to keep your body strong. They will taste like pure life and like growth and survival. They will give you all the vitamins you need. The best gift a friend can give me is something they have grown in their garden or window herb pots. Learn about vegetables. They each have their own special secrets and gifts, their own recipe for energy. They will help your bowels function and warm your brain to process the mayhem that has become your life in the death club.

We live in an agricultural society. Our first president was a great farmer. Many of them were for that matter. Take full advantage of the choices out there. I eat with the harvest. By that I mean I buy what is plentiful and inexpensive. Frozen vegetables are partially dead and canned are almost completely dead. The fresh ones hold all of their vitamins just under the surface and often on their skin, ready for you to heal yourself. They will help to combat the toxins in your system and restore your color.

Organic vegetables are sometimes cost prohibitive but you can learn ways around this. Let everyone in your support system know you are a vegetable whore and they will find them for you. There may be people you work with or go to church with that what love to share their vegetable wealth with you. It gives people great pleasure to give their treasures grown in their yards and brag to you about how they have the best of something you will ever eat. Let them brag, praise their produce!

You may be lucky enough to have access to farmers markets and produce stands. These procurers of produce always have a deal and will be honored to bestow their vegetable wisdom. There are many great books on the use and value of vegetables. Find one at a health food store or bookstore and put it next to your bible. Nutrition is the key to health. You body is a machine that when fueled properly will do the work it is asked to do. Learning to understand the medicinal and antioxidant use of vegetables will be a great service to your grocery shopping trips.

If you have access to a great nutritionist or naturopathic doctor they will be able to tell which veggies have which vitamins. They may also be able to tell which may not go well with your particular symptoms or medications. It is a science and should be used to save you from unnecessary weight loss or discomfort. I won't lie to you, they may cause you extra gas or rumbling so choose carefully depending on how you feel.

I have spent considerable time in the last thirteen years learning about food and how it works. It is a shame it took me until I was sick to really pay attention. Vegetables are a wonderful pure gift from the earth and sun and can cleanse your body better than no other. I worship them and have loved learning how to cook them. Oh, by the way, fruit rates just as high. Bring it along for the ride.

PILLS

Once in a while you forget you are sick; for just a few minutes. Then it is pill time.

Pills, pills, pills. The bane of our existence. In the death club you live in a world of small objects that hover like constellations around every meal and the planning of every day. These tiny, or not so tiny objects that seem to know just where to go and just what to do once they get into your stomach.

Getting them there is the nightmare. First you have to get them prescribed and to the pharmacy. The authorizations and insurance battles are endless and harrowing. Then you out-of-pocket or co-pay yourself into poverty just getting them home to the kitchen. Then you spend hours counting and boxing and dividing just to get them close to a glass of water. Then when the time is right and you think you get them down without heaving you take them.

It's over. They are in. It is time to laugh. That is when the hell may really begin. The down time while you try to choke in a few crackers or some cereal to keep from heaving them back up. Then there is that mystical problem of how to take the empty stomach pills with the food on stomach pills all before an eight-thirty work day. Nausea is imminent at some point with some med or another. It doesn't always hit when you plan either. It may wait until you are on the escalator to the subway, or you are in the middle of a sales meeting, or worst of all, at the meat counter in the grocery store.

If the nausea doesn't hit you are probably going to experience some other gastro-intestinal attack. You may have pain or cramps or loose bowels. Just remember that these little bombs you swallow are going to cure you, if they don't kill you first.

Side effects, drug interactions, damage to other systems in your body not targeted by the medications, all possible casualties. You start taking pills to stop the damage of the pills you are taking to stop the damage of the pills you are taking.

Pills in the morning, the afternoon, the evening, during the night. Fucking pills. Damned pills!

Lovely pills. Some pills are lovely. The one that takes the pain away. The one that gets your appetite back. The one that helps you get up and face the world. The one that works. Pills will become a part of your existence. You will have to make room for them in your world. They will go on vacation with you, to the mall, to work. They will worry you and stress you as they start to run out. They will make you dependent on them.

They will possess you and you will have to surrender to them and make your piece, until your next pharmacist consultation. Learn about your pills and make them part of your power. Make them less than they seem and let them do more than you hope. Pills are pills. They have a job. They will help you to be well, or at the very least, comfortable.

QUICKENING

Being a player in the death club you will experience a quickening. A feeling of understanding and knowing about things you never dreamt you would contemplate. This quick growth process will begin with the day you get your diagnosis and you are coming home from the clinic.

You will suddenly see everything from a strange pair of glasses fitted so tightly to your head that your ears will bleed. This new enlightenment will overwhelm you with fear or tears or joy when you least expect it. I had an episode one day in front of the Air and Space museum. I was approaching the steps and a person who was obviously very sick was begging for money. At once they were me and I was this person. Everyone walked past trying not to see them. They were invisible. So was I . We were invisible together. The members of the club are often invisible. We march along silently hiding behind our glasses and our baggy clothes to hide our wasting. We sit on the bus with each other, wait at the doctors together. We are playing miniature golf with our nephew at some cheesy theme park.

We are alive and struggling and present. We are full of love and pain and hope. We are knowing the truth and seeing the future. We are seeing the good in the smallest can of soda or the simple white pillow case. We are praying for each other and carrying our banners in the light, plain to see to us; invisible to all others.

We suddenly know that our best friend should leave her husband and that the pregnant lady in line at the bank is going to have a girl. What do we do with this quickening? This ability to see through the shame and stupidity to know the simplest thing that matters more than any other.

John F. Green

This is our gift. Our immaculate reward. Our brass ring. It gives us the power, not the right, to speak the truths of the universe and to know our own. We will see the connection of all living things and admire its beauty in a light that will shine in us for all others to recognize. We will really know joy, fear, and love. We will laugh aloud at the worst joke and cry over the smallest wrong doing. We will feel the pain of the universe and know the pleasure of the truth. We will find the strength to speak out about things we suddenly know to be true and not fear the consequences of our actions.

We are going to die and it just doesn't matter anymore. What matters is, what is the most real; a perfect day, a great movie, a piece of cake with lemon frosting. Children will look at us like angels with their innocent hearts knowing that we know the secrets they just left in the before-life.

People in our lives will tell us that we have a beautiful energy and as afraid as they are of our death they will want our understanding of life. We will dance in the glow of the moon and be free like we have never been free before. Clear and glowing and perfect in our quickening.

ZOOS

We all have been to the zoo. When I was a child I loved to go and see the exotic creatures moving to and fro in their cells of iron and cement. I loved to hold my fathers hand and be afraid and safe as the lion roared to me and bared its huge sharp teeth. I loved to have cotton candy and peanuts and a balloon that ultimately escape my grasp.

Now I hate the zoo. It pains me to see the animals trapped for their own survival from extinction in their simulated environments. I hate it because I am in my own death club zoo. The members know where the zoo really is. It is at the family party where everyone surmises your death status and says their polite and lovely and seemingly kind things thinking they are being human.

28

It isn't their fault that they don't understand the patronizing looks and the sympathy. They don't see the iron bars that surround us as we sit in our chair off to the side safe from flying balls and the real laughter. They don't see that the smile on our face is paint and that behind it we cry inside wishing to just be free like them and be able to go recklessly forward into the day and night loving and hoping and dreaming without the grim reaper holding his shining sickle over our heads.

The zoo is an ugly place with cold bars and bedpans and turnstiles that only move in one direction. The oblivion of desperate, empty cold cement in the night and the hissing from cages nearby. Will the python escape and strangle me in my sleep? Will the hyena laugh its eerie threat into the darkness and leave me trembling and cold and afraid?

I can kill the lion and the hyena. I can slay the serpent python. I can leave the zoo and never look back. All I need is for all of them to look at me through the bars and see me for what I really am. A tiger with golden stripes and big eyelashes or a monkey on a branch swinging with delight that the zoo keeper is bringing yellow bananas and fresh water. All they have to see is that I am alive in my cage and real and warm and breathing as I always have. I may look pale and withered but I am not. I am a tiger. I am a monkey. I am a man.

ADMISSION

What will I admit?   Who will I admit?   What is my admission?

To excise the disease from my body I must be able to face the things that I have done and cast them out through penance or recompense or love. Just love what I have done and hate what I have done and be clear of the difference. I must purge the days of abandonment and embrace those of goodness.

Admit me to myself. Admit me to the room in the hospital and let me heal and be healed. Admit to myself that I am frail and that I will need to go to a room in a big building and let people put things in me to hurt me and heal me at once. A simultaneous confusion of syrups and potions and x-rays

31

that will haul out the mire in my damaged tissue and cleanse it to begin anew.

I will admit that I am wrong. I have been wrong. I will admit that I have loved and dreamt and cared and cried and prayed and that all of these things are mine to admit. I will admit you in to my heart to love me and bring me comfort and tell me that you are afraid for me and that you are going to cry when I leave you.

We will be able to admit our humanity to each other and praise our precious time and know that all is perfect in the sky today. We will sing and scream and cry together and be of another world. We will admit ourselves to grieve for our own loss and our own shortcomings. We will admit we could have done better and that we want to do better. And we will beg to bargain with God if he will hear our confession just to buy a few more weeks or days or minutes.

Then forgiveness will be in our sight and we will know that we have done the job and we will have remission and joy and time. Precious time.

REMISSION

The word that is crystal. The death row pardon. Never too late, never too clear. "You are in remission", they will say and your heart will come alive and you will rejoice. You will cry and pray and be happy and run to the people you love and share your happy day of freedom and growth.

The sheer power of this wonderful brilliant word will give the strength to paint the fence and plant a tree and cook the best damn spaghetti in all the free worlds. You will plan a new day and know it will come and think about getting your hair cut again.

Even if it is a temporary lie you will not care. You will be too busy thinking about Christmas and getting back to work and ice cream. Remission will be the catalyst of new ideas and you will zoom in your quickening and be lit inside with a fresh pot of teeming sparkling hot oil.

The word so constructed to mean so much to you when you need its rescue. Re-mission. The mission will begin again. All of the missions will begin again. The missionary of self will be preserved for another day or week or year. A new baby will be allowed to be born for you. A new leaf will come after the fragrant blooms on your orange tree and the oranges will be harvested by your hand.

The beach will seem so clean as the sand finds its way through your toes and the salty water rushes in to greet you. The dolphins will leap high to chirp your name aloud for everyone to hear. You will have sanctity and light and peace again. Remission will be yours to hold in your bosom and languish long into the night with your lifes loves holding your newly strengthened arms.

John F. Green

The day will be clear and the school bus will gleam and be beautiful as it stops to gather you for another trip to school. Math will be easy and music class will rejuvenate your immunity and the hair on your arm will stand as the pledge of allegiance is for you. For you. You and your beautiful gift of Remission.

COOKIES

Cookies with secret fortunes and words of wisdom. Cookies with chocolate chips and nuts and sugar. Pure beautiful god like cookies. Cookies for every day and special occasions. Love those cookies.

When my grandmother heard a friend of hers was dying and couldn't eat to many things she baked her a batch of butter cookies. These pancake like wafers of sugar and flour, and butter that melt on your tongue. They were full of healing love and deepest concern. They sustained her friend and brought her soured taste a moment of peace and tenderness. They helped her to be able to tolerate her time in her bed with crumbs everywhere and that no one bothered about.

Let people bring you cookies. Bake them yourself. Buy them all at the bakery and lay on them on the floor and eat your way to fatness and pleasure. Share them with your children and your lovers and the dog.

Cookies are the fruit of pleasure and kindness and bakers hands. Hail the bakers. Hail the cookies. Eat them. Fill yourself with cookies and be strong and wiry from their sugar and chocolate. Bring some to the hospital to bargain for better care. Bring some to the support group and share their magic macadamia madness. Bring one in your pocket to eat on the way home from chemo. Cookies are the symbol of youth and lustful dietary redemption. Cookies are peace in a small round coin that can buy anything you will ever need. The currency of happy times.

Thank you cookie creators. Thank you cookies.

LAW

The universe is full of laws. The law that all things will at some point die. We are part of that inescapable law. How we negotiate that law and choose to interpret it is our power. Will we surrender at the first notice and collapse into the universe to await our rebirth? Will we say no and take a few more years to pay the bill?

Let the universe take you to collections. Defy it with all your soldiers and slingshots. Throw mud balls in its face and say no! You can't have me yet. I am not done. I am alive and glowing and fragrant like a flower that has just opened. I will blossom and then wither and you will wait for me to be done. Ignore the second notice and the phone calls and the late fees. Steal the time and don't look back. The law is an ass. Dickens was right.

Take what you need and know that it won't ever be more than you should take. That can't happen because the universe is perfect. It knows when to let go and let you breathe and be real and take care of the lovely grass in the back yard. The universe will let you finish everything that you start in the best way you can. It will hear your lawyer defend your case and be patient with the cross examination. The universe is a fair and gentle prosecutor. It is the law and the law is good.

Don't be afraid to break it. To take as much time as you need. That alone is the real truth. You will have the time you need to the last second. The law will not preclude your work or let you go unfinished. The dove may seem to come to the window just a minute too soon but it will not. You will be done. You will have what you need. Don't fret and wring your hands in fear of the chariots arrival. It won't be early. It won't be late. It is the law. You are the law.

INCLUSION

Include everyone. It is the right of the law of the interaction of all that we are. We are everyone we love and they are us. We are integrated and included. We belong to each other and must have our work done together.

Include your childhood friend Margie and your ex-husband Joe. Include the lady at the bank that always asks after you. Include the Rabbi and the Priest. Include the lady next door and the man at the dry cleaners. They are all you and you are them. We are all part of the awareness that keeps us alive and healthy.

Be of substance and strength and solidity. Be whole and loved and dimensional. Include yourself in the scheme of the lives around you and they will include you. Today you are a part of a thousand lives and tomorrow you are part of a million more. Be included in the beating of those hearts and let them carry you forward. Join the team. Play the game and be included. Nothing can stop you but your own fear to be a part. Be included and live and prosper and heal. Be a part of the whole resonant energy that already exists around you. Let it sing through you and feel it with warmth and acceptance. Be included.

HOPE

All that there is. Hope. I want to have hope and I do. Hope for me and I will hope for you. When you name a child Hope, you make the world a better place. When you say the word out loud, I hope you feel better. You give the universe a chance to react to your thoughts. That single word sets the gears moving. All the angels say someone just hoped and now we will have to get on the situation. They proceed immediately to the machinery and turn it to high and make everything happen.

Hope for me that I will breathe tomorrow and I will hope the same for you. Hope that my test results will show improvement and they will. I have a dear Aunt that bases her whole life on hoping for other people and all her hope is dispersed to us for our sanctity and might. She just sends it out without any condition and it comes back around again and again. She got the message. Let us heed her example and hope very clearly.

I have a friend named Hope and she is the very discernable. Her parents gave her a name to remind her every day of how to be in the world of people and things and animals. She just listens to her name and jumps to action. She brings her hopefulness to the success of everyone she meets. She is the creature of hope.

When you go to your doctor say, " I hope this will be good news." Say, " I hope I will be more well." Say, " I hope this will be a day of triumph for me". And if it isn't, hope that tomorrow will be. It is that easy.

Don't be afraid to hope for everything you want for yourself and everyone you love. Teach them all to hope with you. It is that easy. That simple. That perfect. Take it into your heart and use it to your best success. I hope you will. I hope I will.

EXTRAORDINARY

Extra. Ordinary. Not ordinary at all. You will rise to the occasion on more than one occasion. You will be extraordinary. When you least expect it, with your pants on a hook and an IV in your arm and your ass exposed to everyone on Three East you will be so extraordinary.

The nurses will pause and the techs will screech to a halt and the orderly will stop mopping and pearls will shoot out of your mouth and shower down on everyone and the universe on Three east will stop and listen to you. Just to you and you alone. You, the extraordinary one.

Your pain will not matter. Your skinny body will have no countenance. Your naked ass will not compromise a single adverb. You will be a voice. Clear and resonant and prophetic.

You will sing the meaning of the universe in Egyptian and Portuguese and street and everyone will hear. Their ears will twist hard and fast and glue to your tongue and draw in the breath you release and they will be enlightened by you. It will be your moment. Your time of eloquent, splendorous, philosophical verbiage salads. Your pronouns and verbs and adjectives will cascade unmodified by the spirit of your pure self and all will listen. They will all listen to you. Being extraordinary.

They will take you home inside their souls and deliver you to their husbands and children with warm affection. They will tell the Pastor and Elaine at the beauty shop and Ted the guy at the florist. They will think of you on their pillows and eat you with their yogurt. You will be with them for days as they decipher the riddles and truths and commandments you spoke to them and they will be changed forever.

They will be changed like you because for a moment just in their hall, on Three east, you were extraordinary.

LUCID

Will I remain lucid? When I am dying, will I remain lucid?
Will the words coming out of my mouth mean anything?
Will I know to care? I want to be cognizant of my departure.
I want to be clear and lucid.

We hear people say this phrase on medical shows all the
time, is he lucid? We don't really know what that means,
do we? Does that mean present to hear what is being said
and to understand it; or does it mean conscious? I think I
was not lucid on a recent trip to the hospital for severe food
poisoning. One minute I was present and communicative
and then people were moving around me and saying things
and everything seemed like it was in slow motion and so
distant from me, despite that I was the center of attention.

When I came to, some hours later I realized that I had collapsed and traveled far away from the place they were working on me to protect my spirit from the fearful actions and manipulations that were my treatment at that moment. I was safely distant. Safely disconnected.

Sometimes we get so ill that we have to be given extreme amounts of pain medication and we lose our lucidity. This again is a combination of chemical and spiritual things going on simultaneously to protect us from the truth of our situation. It is not a bad place to be in my opinion. As we ready ourselves to leave we must have times of detachment to begin our separation from the physical plain. This isn't a bad thing at all. It is also not a definitive thing. If we decide not to leave we can come back and be well. Well we can recover from this distance sometimes and come back to the room and be present again.

When we have been sick and then we are very lucid we can have the most wonderful rejuvenation. We can really enjoy popcorn and the Bee-Gees album in the hall closet and the sound of the rain on the tin roof. We can sit in our lucidity in a chair in the living room for hours and listen to everything around us and absorb it in absolute detail to use when we least expect to.

When we are lucid we can make phone calls and negotiate with the gas company and write a little note to LoLo in Montreal. We can go see a movie and have lunch with Roberta our massage practitioner. When we are lucid we can write our will and decide to whom to give our Grandmothers china. We can sing an entire song we learned in third grade for the May Procession at church. We can balance the checkbook and do that little two step our friend Marie taught all of us in college.

Most importantly, when we are lucid we know who Marie is. Who Roberta and LoLo are. We know that our husband is our husband and that the cats name is Chelsea. We know that we are present. Present and lucid.

PROMISES

Make a promise. Promise to keep it. Keep it forever. I promise I will love you. I promise I will talk to the doctor about that. I promise I will get out of bed today and take a shower. Promises can be kept. They can be made. They can be honored. And if they aren't it doesn't matter at all. The ones that are meant to survive will and the rest will be released in forgiveness.

When other people make promises to you let them know you will hold them accountable. Let them know that you will expect delivery. Don't make a promise to a dying man and then fail to keep it. A broken promise is the worst kind of karmic poop you can leave on the carpet. Let them know they don't have to make a promise.

Why bother. Who cares? Make a wish for me instead. If a wish doesn't come true nobody gets hurt. Promises are a whole different ball game. They are sacred and bonding and all of that really entrenched stuff that holds over for a millennium in some big freezer on the ethereal plain.

Give me a wish over a promise. Give me a box of candy for that matter. Give me your heart and your smiles and your tender touch. Give me a ride to the grocery store on a really hot day in your big air-conditioned car. Give me anything, but avoid making me a promise.

I don't need promises. They just set me up for disappointment. If you want to promise to think about me every day for the rest of your life I'll take it. If you want to promise to tell my son how much I loved him I'll take it. If you want to, promise to look for me in heaven. Promise to remember me in your heart like a balloon on a string and pull me in when you need me close. Promise to cry for me when you miss me and promise to laugh at all my idiosyncrasies as long as you can remember them. Promise to take my picture with you through your life and put it on the bookcase in the den so I can visit you when you have the time to visit me.

If I can't promise you anything and you can't promise me anything we will still be fine. Promises get broken. They fall off the back of the sofa and through the crack in the floor and are forgotten. Then they haunt us like the questions on the history test that we just couldn't remember. When you make a promise the recipient takes it to heart so make sure you can deliver the goods. Your doctors will think they can get away with using the word promise all the time. Silly fools. Reckless insolent disembodied pill pushers. How dare they? God doesn't even make promises. The only promise that is truly realized is the promise to die. We will eventually. I promise.

SURVIVE

To survive suggests victimization. There is a victim that survives. There is a wrong doing that you beat. There is a downfall that has been up-righted. I'm not a victim. I'm not righting anything. I am just living with a situation called AIDS and I have to work to change that. I will not have to survive AIDS because I am not dying from AIDS. You will not have to be a cancer survivor because you don't have cancer. Part of your body has cancer. Part of your heart is broken. Part of the fence is down.

It isn't about surviving. It is about mending. It is about finding the strength to go on to the next day and get the therapy and take the pill and have the radiation. Buying a wig isn't surviving it is buying a wig. Buy groceries

55

on Tuesday, buy a new shirt on Wednesday, buy a wig on Friday. Buy some time on Saturday.

Don't survive, live. Act. Dance. Sing. Go to work and eat dinner and pay the cable bill and go visit your sister in Rochester. Don't survive. Victims survive. We aren't victims. We are people that are sick and need to heal. We are not diseased; the tissue in our body is diseased. We are whole and perfect as we always have been. I happen to have a little bit of AIDS today and you have a little Cancer. Screw it, don't give it the power.

Don't survive, heal. Heal your pancreas and your blood and your breasts and your lymphatic system. Heal the dog from fleas and the plant on the balcony from aphids. We are not victims, we are artists and teachers and bus drivers and administrative assistants. We are dancers and carpenters and airplane pilots. We aren't victims though, not now, not ever. Victims are victimized. I am not victimized, I'm healing. You are not victimized, you are healing.

HANDS

Take my hand. Take my hand in yours. Take my hand in marriage.. Hold my hand. Hold my pulse close to yours. Let me feel safe. Let me feel loved. Walk with me hand in hand. Let me feel your hand and arm swinging back and forth with mine. Let your simple appendage with four perfect fingers and a thumb, dangling loose connected to mine feed my lonely soul. Let the beach draw us along as we chase a piece of discarded Styrofoam floating on the surf. Let us follow it for miles and miles and let our hands stay together. Our friendship and companionship tethered and entwined and happy together.

Hands are our self in miniature. They show others all of our innocence and pain and hard work and bad cooking accidents and the length of our life line. They show if we have time to take care of ourselves or if we are rushed and pressured to work hard. They tell the Natura-path if we are well or lacking. They tell the doctor if we are dehydrated or cold from poor circulation.

They wave about when we talk and help us tell our stories. They reveal our heritage and mimic our fathers and mothers. They talk for us when we are mute. They dress us and feed us and open the door for us. Our separate hands that link us to each other in chains.

Our perfect hands that let us caress each other and give each other wonderful sweet orgasms. Our hands that fit into gloves when we are cold and into dark wholes in the earth to plant bulbs to grow us spring blooms. Our nimble fingers that weave baskets and sort pills and paint pictures and pare potatoes. Our nails that get bitten to indicate our fear and get polished to show our refinement.

We have two. Why not four. Who could we hold, what could we make? Hold the baby and pet the dog. Play two violins and drive while playing poker. No, just two. For you to hold and make me feel safe. Two to clap for the band and swing on the jungle gym. Just two to fit into a pocket on each hip. One to hold the toothbrush and one to wipe the steam off of the mirror. The two in joyous synchronicity carrying a birthday cake into the room while the mouth sings that silly little song. My hands and your hands; and all the hands in Mrs. Rideouts' third grade class making shadow puppets on the wall. One to lift the plant out of the window while the other lowers the blind.

One to wipe a tear from my cheek while the other pats me gently. Two to reach around me and pull the blanket onto my shoulders. One to hold the vile and the other the syringe. Two hands working in tandem massaging my pained feet. Two silky hands lifting a glass to my lips when I am too weak to reach for it myself. Two hands carrying the compassion you feel for me from your heart to my face. Mine holding

John F. Green

onto them for dear life. Dear, dear life. Life in my hands,
in your hands.

SENTENCE

What is our sentence? We are sentenced to death. We are sentenced to suffer. We are sentenced to life. We take our sentence and sanction our terms and negotiate our presence to be known by God and our very own selves.

The sentence we dare to listen to as our doctor speaks it. Our prognosis demonic and looming and freeing and poignant and frightful. Our bargain with God degreed. Our pregnant pause that goes to tears and mayhem and calamity and peace. Our listening heart screaming in pain and anguish. The truth we know and deny so.

The sentence to go on with what we have and take those horrid pills every day. The sentence to keep paying the car payment even though we may never see it paid off. The sentence to keep watering the grass so we won't lose resale that day we relinquish it to another owner who won't remember us at all. The sentence to pray for parole each day we have the chemo.

Take the vitamins, eat the carbohydrates, floss. Wax the car, get the oil changed, clean out the garage. Wash the floor, take out the trash, iron the shirt. Pay for the plot, choose the casket, pick out the headstone. Be born, live your life, die with grace.

The sentence to get the blood work, go to the support group, sit in the room with the strangers. To smell the smell of our own urine in our bed and just let go of it. The sentence to have a good day as a tease before three bad ones. To cry at a stupid movie and hide in the dark watching the cars go by our window. To smell a flower and remember the fourth of July with fireworks and bands and crowds in the park on picnic blankets oohing and aahing in unison. Us apart of the whole. The whole knowing we are leaving to fulfill our sentence.

The universe being silent and still as we hover above it in a beam of light moving to the hand of our grandmother as she smiles ahead to show us the path to heaven.

The sentence in our first grade primer that says, see Spot run. Who is Spot? Why is he running? To avoid the inevitable sentence. To escape the speeding car, to chase the ball, to catch the dog next door. Run Spot run. Run, run, run. Run from the sentence that lingers in our ears like the criminal breath of fate. Run from the disease that will wither your energy and take your breath as you speak your last. Your very last. Sentence.

WHOLE

Be a part. Be whole. Dig a hole and then fill it in and walk away. Holes are a place of lack; whole is without lack. Choose the one with the W. You are whole and perfect. You are born with everything you need to know and you spend your whole life forgetting the truths you came with. Don't forget. Don't lose any part of the whole.

Holistic is the connection of mind, body and spirit. Let them float and be connected upon you. Bring them together and lash them so tightly together that you are unshakeable.. Be strong and pure and whole. Know the difference. Be the space between the needle and the thread. Sew your skin to your muscle and your blood to your veins. Cleanse your life and your shoeboxes of all the ticket stubs and just remember the play.

Dance in the grocery store and talk to lady in line at the bank. Smell the bacon in the kitchen and drink all the water it takes to quench the salty thirst left behind. Eat watermelon and pee for a long time. Be whole in your skin and shine like a new penny. Copper and infinite and brazen with Lincolns face reminding you to free the slaves and be emancipated. Emancipated and whole. All your parts linked like train cars speeding along, brisk and flowing in the universe of tracks and crossings.

Whole in the knowing of the names of all the fathers and all the mothers that made you whole. Whole in the moonlight and the rays of the radiation machine and the lab results. Hole in the pocket that lets your penknife slip to the floor and lose your lucky rabbit foot. Whole in knowing that it's only a penknife and a rabbits' foot and that rabbits breed like knives are manufactured.

Whole days and whole nights looming before you like crystals on a chandelier in a ballroom with wooden floors and room to dance around and around without ever hearing the music. Whole lives that connect together like pearls on a string waiting to be broken into parts. They will never really be parts. They can't because they are whole.

SILENCE

Silent. Quiet. Silence is golden. Silence is you with
yourself. Me with myself, silent. Knowing, listening,
feeling, remembering, silent. The absence of sound. The
calm before the storm. Still and present and silent.

The sound of just your heart beating and the IV dripping
and the clock ticking and the ocean breaking on the shore
beyond you while you are silent. Say nothing, do nothing,
be nothing. Empty and sure of fulfillment. Silent and radiant
and smiling and thinking and loving and being tender inside.
Silent and aware and frightened and ready.

Silent and listening for the movement to begin and the gun
to fire and the deer to collapse into the snow and bleed out

to you. Silent as you draw in your breath and wince as they shove that thing in your throat and look into your gut to see the disease that you are praying will have receded silently. Silent as the nurse slides the IV needle from your arm and presses a cotton pad hard to clot you and you heave a sigh of relief that it is over until Thursday.

Silent as the moon and the dawn that will bring the light back to your room on the third floor. Your room where you go to be silent and read the letter from Jill who went to school with you. Jill who ran in the woods with you when you were eleven. Jill who walked to the bus with you each day for six years of school. Walking with Jill in silence. Sometimes you talked and laughed. You talked about homework and the kids on the bus and what you were doing in Algebra. You talked about babysitting and buying new record albums on the weekend at the record store. You talked about the episode of that show when the lady had cancer and how tragic it was and that she died. You talked about being afraid of band tryouts and finishing that paper for English Lit. She knew your secrets and you knew hers and you could be silent together.

When you are not silent you should be very loud. Very clear of what you shouldn't remain silent about another minute. Speak to the birds and your cat and the man that sweeps the hall on Monday morning. Speak to the truths you hold so tightly in your heart. Speak of your loves and your hates. Speak to your lover and whisper their name aloud to yourself on the bus. Speak to your mother on mother's day and tell her how much you enjoyed the last visit. Speak the names of all your pills like a chant as you take them to kill that evil disease you really don't need anymore.

Speak Spanish and French and tell stories to your kids in Pig Latin. Speak the words of the Lords prayer and listen to your own voice being answered by just God alone. Speak to the injustices in the universe and the high tax bill. Speak to the quality of the antique chair you're buying on Saturday. Speak to the girl behind the counter at the ice cream parlor and tell her all your wishes for the waffle cone and the sprinkles. Speak to the X-ray guy because he wants to listen to your life while he takes a picture of the heart that beats behind your voice.

Speak out to hopefulness and healing. Call your lovers name again and let him come to your side and hold your hand and be with you. Comforting you with his tender voice. Or better yet just sit together in silence.

LINGERING

Lingering thoughts. Lingering residue of nicotine on your finger tips. Linger in the lobby at the hotel to see who comes and goes. Linger in the hall for a moment longer to look at the children through the door fast asleep. Linger in the night with your lovers arms wrapped around your shoulders breathing in and out on your back, asleep and angelic and warm. Linger your fingers in his hair or on her brow.

Never linger at the hospital just get the hell home. To your place of lingering sunny days by the big rose bush that is growing over the garage roof. Daylight lingering time and the taste of lemon in your mouth after the cake is finished. Linger a little late from lunch with Susan and Ginny and talk about that guy Susan met at the gym and let them dock you.

John F. Green

You will know the secret stolen moments that linger in your memories like precious stones and ocean breezes. Waiting to manufacture peace of mind and stability and fortify your memory with happy times and great laughs. Laughs you'll need when your doctor is lingering in the hall outside the door answering a page and you're shitting yourself worrying about your white blood cell count.

Allow the dinner to linger in the oven while you kiss on the sofa in the den. Let the smell of your boyfriend's cologne linger in your nose and the smell of his sweat linger on your stomach. Let the bouquet he sent linger on your dressing table until it is completely dry.

Let your heart linger with lust over the guy at the car wash. Let your laughter linger in the night on the back porch to disturb all the neighbors. Let the broken glass linger in the alley to catch the light when the sun hits it right. Let your teeth linger on a piece of gristle from the juiciest steak you've ever eaten. Let a pomegranate's juice linger on your sleeve long enough to make a crimson stain. Wear the stain with pride. Remember that pomegranate every time you linger in that comfortable cotton shirt.

Lingering spirits will seek you out to accompany them to heaven. Don't linger with them. Linger on the moon and look back to the Earth and freeze the sight of it in your memory forever. You will need to find the way back. Hurry back. Don't linger.

ADVENTURE

What an adventure. Take this adventure with me. Come along for the ride. Experience the adventure. Where will we go and what will we do? An adventure to the store or the bank. One to the doctor or the pharmacy? An adventure to the basement for an X- ray. The blood work and the CT scan, all adventures to be experienced.

A much needed vacation with a cherished friend. The way home from your life in another place. Your life itself. All adventures to challenge you and keep you guessing. Where will you go next; will it be an easy trip? My fearful adventure for the eye implant. Yours for the chemo. Our adventures together at the waiting room in the clinic. Watching everyone else in the club having their own adventures.

The first visit to the disability office at the Social Security building. The trip to the bank to close your savings because it is empty. The trip to the pawn shop. Back to the pawn shop. The trip to the grocery store with food stamps for the first time. The trip to your parents with a new diagnosis. What will you say? What will they do? It will be a trip for sure.

Adventures every day with trial medications and no safe guards. Venturing out into the night with no energy just to be with other people and have a drink at the local bar. Venturing to the grocery store in one hundred degree heat when you feel like hell to begin with just to get some Immodium and Gatorade. Venturing into the video rental store to find the same movies you just saw last week. Venturing into the lab to have your arm poked and bleed a little for the chemists.

What adventures lay ahead? Where will you go? Where will you be able to go? Where will you want to go? What will you want to seek? Will it be there? Adventure forth with the best laid plans and take the trip of your life. Even if it be your last.

ADVOCATES

The defender of truth and justice and fair play.   The advocate.   See them all.   The one who goes the distance on your behalf.   You advocating for yourself.   Fighting the bank and the health insurance company and the disease itself. The wretched enemy dashed on the rocks due to advocacy. The truth told.   The voice heard; the song sung.   The difference between success and failure.   The representation of knowledge.   The fear dispelled.

The doctor that makes the call.   The nurse that goes to the second floor to get the ginger-ale out of the lounge soda machine.   The man that lets you go ahead of him at the grocery store.   All advocating for your comfort and wellness and peace.   All carrying you on their shoulders like a huge flag for all to take notice. The congressman that fights for the reform, the dog that leads the blind man. All advocates. All saviors of our plight and weaknesses. The finders of strength, the wishers of wellness, the creators of righteousness. The one that explains the form, spells the word. The one that rescinds the overdraft fee. The one that handles you with tender touches when the skin is raw. The kind gentle one that holds the glass. The one that changes the sheets and puts the dinner tray close enough to you because they know you can't rise for it. The one that thinks ahead for you on the hot day and has the specimen cup at the front desk. The one that brings the car up to the door and has the heat going full blast. The post man that puts the mail inside the storm door so you don't have to come out on the porch. The minister that comes to see you at home. Your dear Aunt Peggy who asks for masses in your name and sends you articles on new treatments. Your mother who stuffs a twenty in your pocket when the end of the month is near. All wonderful advocates. All there for you on the worst day with your weakest heart. All loving you in their own unique and different ways. All fighting for your life so you can become strong and be their advocate another day.

ANGER

Get angry and then let it go. Stay angry all day if you need to. Turn it loose. Set it free. It will take your time and tense your neck and deplete your chi. Say goodbye to the anger. Work it out, scream it out, let it go. Let it go. I said let it go. That is all you do. Take the power out of it. Just be happy instead. Don't let the anger take your days. I know you are angry. I am angry. I don't want to do this anymore. I hate everything. I hate the doctor and the hospital and the bank and the pills. Oh how I hate the pills.

Anger and rage, rage and hollering and screaming and then quiet. You will be sorry after the anger. It will take something from you that you can't get back. Don't let it. Just say,

"Anger, anger, go away!" Just hurl a glass off the back porch and let it all go. It doesn't matter. It doesn't have anything to do with anything. It never does. It is just a feeling of powerlessness. A feeling of weakness and confusion. Anger is not about wrong doing. It is about powerlessness. Take back your power. Be powerful over your disease. Lead it to where you want it and kill it in a dark alley. Not with anger but with love. Reach inside and grab it and yank it out of yourself and stomp it to death. Kill the disease. Then take all the anger and throw it in the dumpster with the disease in a big plastic bag and leave it for forensics.

Anger is sorrow; it is fear. Anger is the rotten food in the fridge and the dirt on the car floor. It is the grease you bring in from the garage and the mud puddle at the end of the block. It is all the muck and mire in the universe from lack and wanting and hate and confusion. Anger is the weakness in our heart and the laziness to work it out using our brains and our eyes and voices and hands. Anger is the dog shit on your good shoes. It just is. You bet your life it is. So let it go.

John F. Green

Say goodbye to it. Goodbye anger. Goodbye fear. Goodbye confusion and hate. Bye anger. Don't come back.

CARPET

Pile of fibers twisted tightly together holding dust mites and buttons and coins and straight pins from the new shirt. Backed with rubber, nailed to the floor. Loose and sliding and wrinkled by the back door. Carpets of blue and chartreuse and red. Carpets going up the stairs and down the hall. Carpet covering the cracks in the floor and the peeling linoleum. Irresistible plush pile to lie on and watch a movie and read a book. Carpet to smell like you and the dog and the fried flounder from last Tuesday.

Carpets of flowers on the back lawn. Carpets of oranges and tomatoes and yellow corn at the farmers market. Carpets of towels on the sale table at Macy's. Carpets into churches and up museum entrances. Carpets in cars to keep the metal from feeling hot or cold. Gum on the carpet at the movie theater and ketchup on the restaurant carpet. Fields of carpet in the stores along the mall holding carpets of things to buy and fondle and dream about. The carpet under the Porsche in the showroom.

Carpet in the waiting room and in the elevator. Carpet on the head of the old man in line at the bank. Carpet samples making a patchwork on the basement floor. Wet carpet from the washer overflowing or the heavy rain that got in the side window. Carpet under foot with bare feet and sore ankles. Carpet to suck up the noise of the office machines and halt the screech of sliding chairs. A carpet that is mine passed down for centuries. Carpet under my favorite chair to catch the remote when it slides from my sleeping hand. Carpet to connect me to you with small electric static jolts when we embrace. Carpet to keep my knees from bruising when I crawl upstairs to bed after the chemotherapy. Carpet to play with your daughter and son. A wonderful game of tinker toys or Candyland on that carpet in the family room. A great movie and popcorn on the carpet in the den.

Carpet me with carpets of roses and lily's when I lay in a carpet of taffeta and silk in a carpet of grass at the big cemetery on the hill. Carpet me with licks from the dog. Carpet me with laughter and joy from my little friend Zoe who comes to visit. Carpet my heart with your affection and carpet my immune system with wellness. Carpet the walls and ceilings and every surface in sight with your affection for me. Let me carpet your mind with memories and your face with my kisses. Pick out a color of carpet and put it in my hand. Lush, plush, beautiful carpet.

COMPANY

Come and keep me company. I enjoy the company. Be a part of my company and keep me company. I am in the company, and then I am not. I am in good company. Who is the company that I seek? Will I find them in time? They will be there, I know waiting to keep me in theirs. They will be good company, I hope. I want to enjoy them. I want them not to tire me or take my limited strength. I want them to bring me a pie and a bouquet of flowers. I want them to be the perfect guest and bring their plate to the kitchen after dinner. I want them to stay just the right length of time. I want them to think of me as good company.

Will my company let me go if I can't do my job? Will they offer a disability check to help me through the tough times ahead? Will the members of the company donate time off for me when mine runs out? Will they give me a paycheck when I can't work? Will the people in the office all know what's wrong? Will they want to eat lunch with me? Will they want to keep me in their company?

The company of strangers will become my company. Everywhere I go I will be alone again for the first time, for the last time. I will be in the company of the lady from the bank with her cancer and guy in group with AIDS like me. I will be in the company of others dying and pretending not to. I will know the company that doesn't get a paycheck or a hot meal or a piece of wedding cake. I will be in the company of other dreamers hoping for salvation and emancipation. The lines in our bodies tethering us to machines pumping the drugs from the companies we love and hate simultaneously.

I want to have lots of company. I want the line of mourners to be endless. I want the companies that search for the cures to get busy and be successful and save my fragile ass. I want the company to be kind and friendly and cheerful and busy.

Busy like me seeking the company. Company of friends, company of strangers, just plain old company.

DIFFERENCE

What is the difference? The difference between life or death, truth or lies. Do we really know the difference? Can we? We have to know some differences. We have to take a stance. To know when the treatment is working. To know when we should trust our instincts. To understand the difference between safety and confusion. To choose to understand the difference and act accordingly. To want so much more. To know when we make a difference. To be what we should be and live by our truths and not let anyone convince us that we are wrong even if we are wrong. To take the chance to make the difference we need to make. To be different.

I am different. I am different than you because my life has been different. My days last longer or go faster. My voice is clearer. My temperature is higher. My hands hold things in a different way. My house is different, my clothes, my food. It is all different. Each day is different, each year. I am myself and you are yourself, different than me. We are unique and different. A penny is different from a nickel. Sour is different than sweet. White is different than black. Rain is different than sun. A mountain is different from a valley, each of purpose. One sends the river forth and the other receives it to carry on the plain and the grasses and the trees and eventually the sea. I am the mountain, I am the grass, the tree. You are too, but in a different way. We are different.

Will I feel the difference between the hot and the cold? Will my body respond to this treatment in a different way? Will the disease know my indifference to it and just leave? Will it fight the desertion like an opportunity to grow and attack me in a different way? Why is my immune system different than those of all my friends that have died long before me? What have I done differently? Is luck different from fate, fate from karma, karma from strength, strength from resourcefulness? Resourcefulness from luck?

What is the difference between a red apple and a green one? Some green apples aren't ripe, some are green when they are ripe. Am I a green apple or a red one? Am I ripe if I am green? Will I ever know the difference?

EXPECTATIONS

What should I expect? Expect everything; expect nothing. Don't expect anything. Expect death. It will come. In time it will come. In the mean time expect joy and love. Expect waiting at the doctors and taking pills. Expect your sister to fly in from LA. Expect your birthday to be a little sad and a little happy. Expect your best friend to look at you in a funny way that says I love you and I don't know what I will do without you.

Expect the car payment to be due. Expect the toilet to need a good scrubbing. Expect to get flowers when you are in the hospital. Expect to be glad to get home. Expect to get some bad news from the doctor sometimes. Expect to lose weight. Expect to buy a new dress to show off your skinny ass. Expect to get in your wedding dress and wear it around the house when nobody is home. Expect the Guiding Light to be on in its regular slot. Expect the taste in your mouth to change sometimes and seem a little sour. Don't expect things to taste the same. Some will taste better, some worse. Don't expect to start liking okra just because the Natura-path recommends eating a lot of it. Expect the sun to react to some of your medications.

Expect to see the world in a whole new light. Expect church to seem kind of slow. Expect to get the lesson a little faster. Expect to know why your brother doesn't come to visit as often. Expect some people to not come by at all. Expect that you will forgive them their fear and just love them as you always have. Expect to be angry for a while at first. Don't expect them to come around before it is too late. They will or they won't. You can't expect to change that. It isn't for the changing. It isn't to be expected. Expect to go peacefully. You will if you expect it.

MEMORY

My precious memory. My friend in the night. My companion on a lonely day. My memory. Memories of you. Memories of me and my sister. Memories of Christmas and Easter and the fireman's carnival every summer. Days of sun and the whirly-bird in Mannings back yard. The above ground pool and homemade ice cream, hand cranked with everyone taking a turn. Roller skates and new shoes for school. The beach.

Memories of fights with old lovers and roommates. Fights in the playground at school. The Vietnam war. Cars going fast, past our house in the city. Dogs that scared me on the way to school. The smell of rubber pencil erasers and theme books. The smell of the milk crates waiting in the hall for snack time. My grandmothers bedroom in the apartment in the city with her statues and jewelry boxes. The smell of her perfume on everything mixed with cleaning supplies and furniture polish and moth balls. The light as it filtered through her curtains. Going in to say goodnight to her when we spent the night. In our pajamas and robes, her in her night gown. The three of us kneeling with her and saying prayers and feeling clean and angelic and safe beside her. Her hugs and kisses. The feel of those crisp sheets in the guest bedroom. The feel of her lips on my little cheek, and her arms crushing me to her for absolutely the longest memory minute.

The way the back seat of the Impala looked when I was just five. All the chrome and the blue vinyl. The back of my dad's head with a crew cut or flat top haircut. My mom's scarf blowing as the convertible top accordioned off the car and folded miraculously behind us. The telephone wires above us, the tree tops, the bridges overhead on the way to the city. Clouds. Millions of clouds. Millions and millions.

My velvet jacket. The cover of the Yellow Brick Road album. Don King's hair. Peace signs. Memories of cakes and pies and hamburgers on the grill. Memories of dances and dates and cars and trains. The bakery on the way home from church. My first apartment. My last apartment. The place with all the porches. The one near the harbor. The jeep. All these memories together with me at night. In the morning, in the hospital, at the doctors office waiting to be seen. All these memories being my friend when I feel so lonely and quiet and scared. When nothing is left but me and these memories. Me and these memories.

MIRACLES

Let them come. Let me have miracles. I will be miraculous.
I am miraculous. My birth, my life, my death; all miracles.
I will resonate miraculously in your memory and you will
feel my presence. I am part of the miracles of the universe.
Present and perfect and true. I am a leaf and a dog and a fish
and a miraculously red pomegranate that is filled with blood
and seeds and chambers of seemingly infinite quantity.

A miracle will come. It always does. The money will be
there. The food will be at the store. The gas will be in the
car. The lottery ticket will yield a respite from the money
worries. The day will be miraculously short or as long as
you require. The pharmacist will get the approval for the
refill in miraculous time before the pain starts again. Your

oldest friend will remember your birthday miraculously short of midnight. The tree will fall in the drive instead of on the house. Your office will be flooded on the day you start vomiting from the chemo and you won't have to use sick time. The cake will taste just like you remembered. The dog will catch the ball with miraculous precision one hundred times.

The cantaloupe will be ripe the day you have the strength to carve it into a salad. The sheets will not hold the stains from your incontinence. The vitamins you need will all be on sale. Miracles will happen all around you. Your small reward for the struggle. Your reprieve. You will be in remission on your son's birthday. The train will pass as you reach the crossing. The video you left in the car won't be ruined from the heat. All miracles for you. For you to recognize and celebrate and understand. Miracles of flowers and rainy days when you need them. Miracles of blooming paper whites at Christmas and lots of chocolates in your stocking. Miracles of your friend Charlottes new baby sleeping silently in your arms on the glider on her wooden porch. Miracles of the waves breaking on the beach and you being well enough to go to see them.

Just days full of miracles for you to make up for the days without. Taking away the pain, the fear, the sadness. The lonely days being crushed by pure perfect beautiful miracles. For you and me. For miraculous, incredible, perfect you and me.

NIGHT

The space between days. Rest. Peace. Fearful. Lonely and quiet. Restoration of the liver. Breathing quietly or snoring loudly. Night sweats and fevers. Veins healing. Noses drying, eyes crusting. Tender people sleeping beside us, resting too. Bodies horizontal, heads on pillows. Birds silent in nests. Trucks being loaded for early morning deliveries. Monitors beeping. Nurses taking vitals. Streets empty.

Night. Opposite and dark from days. The sun visiting someone else. The trees storing water to make new leaves while you sleep. Snow not being stepped upon. Cats minding the fort. The electric meter moving slowly. The grass being full of dew. The car's engine cooling off. The refrigerator staying closed. Someone at the convenience store dealing with drunk people. You asleep.

Traveling in dreams to far off places and school rooms from thirty years ago. Your grandmother making an unexpected and much needed visit to see you and play Parcheesee at the kitchen table in her row house. The dog at the foot of the bed. Flying above the mountains with no airplane. The boat at camp taking you to the town beyond. A house with too many rooms that all seem to be in repair. A table full of candy and cakes just for you. No IV in your arm. No phone ringing. No television in the background. No dryer buzzing. Just you and your brain disembodied in travel and joy and sex and flowers and ice cream. Just the smell of the sheets and the gardenia outside your window. You outside of the atmosphere looking back at the earth thinking just how lovely it really can be. You and Jeanne walking on the beach and picking up shells and putting them in a little plastic bucket with the handle still in tact.

John F. Green

Laying awake worrying about the test results. Smelling the fabric softener and being glad you remembered to put it in the wash. Just you and your disease, alone together. Unconscious, conscious, listless, tossing, turning, aching. The foot cramp, the foot asleep. You asleep finally. Recharging, circulating. You in bed. The best place to be sometimes. The place you go to hide. The place that frees you from all other places.

The chair in the den that you sleep in when you can't breathe right. The cool wood floor under your feet when you go to the fridge for a bite of cold potato that you suddenly think you can get down. The late night television and infomercials that annoy you. Home shopping with a credit card that is almost maxed out. Writing in the journal you started for your kids. Your kids asleep and you watching them silently from the hall. Going in to adjust their covers. Something that you alone can still do to provide some care for them. You at night with your thoughts and the sand man in the hall. You sleeping quietly while your husband sets up your morning

IV with you oblivious to the movement. Safe inside yourself at night. The other time from day. The night.

ABOUT THE AUTHOR
by Carol Green

My best friend and brother John F. Green wrote this book. Unfortunately he did not get to complete his thoughts and words because his time ran out. He died on August 4, 2003. I was with him when he left. I was fortunate enough to have had the chance to say my goodbyes to him but then again how can you ever really say goodbye for the last time? How can you speak those words and know that you will never get another chance in this lifetime to hear his voice? To see him smile or cry or hear him laugh and joke about some silly thing he saw on TV just the other day. I am grateful for the 42 years I shared with John, both good and bad. We were as close as a sister and brother can be while growing up, the constant bickering and petty fights of childhood, the difficult adolescent years. Then the growing apart when we both left home.

I think the last four years of his life were probably the best in our relationship. We grew to love each other, respect each other and depend on each other for so many things. He was my pal, my confidant, and best girlfriend. We told each other everything and knew many secrets about each other. I would always seek his advice before making any decisions in my life whether it was a financial matter or contemplating a new lover. I trusted John and had so much admiration for him. We would talk on the phone nearly every day. I would try and be as supportive as I could. Although at times I must admit I just didn't want to be bothered. When I look back on those times I think I must have been a real selfish ass. But it was all part of the process of learning to accept the reality that my brother was sick and dying. As anyone knows who is dealing with or has dealt with a terminally ill loved one, it is a very difficult road. You just want them to get better and get on with their lives. You don't want to have to get up at 3:00 AM and drive over to their house because they called you and said they have a really high fever and need some ice-water and Tylenol and are just to damn sick to get out of bed and get it. Then you wind up getting home 3 hours later and catching a few winks before you have to get up and get ready for work, all the while feeling pissed off at the sick person but knowing that they can't help it and are counting on you to be there.

John was so talented; everything he did was done with careful thought and expertise. He could paint wonderful pictures, write poetry, decorate a house, cook, tell stories, and make everyone laugh. His favorite poet was Emily Dickinson and he used to quote her quite frequently. He was always kind and always had something nice to say to everyone. Even on his bad days, near the end of his illness when he was in excruciating pain, he would bark at the nurses and then asked our mother to bring a box of candy to the nurses so they would know that he was sincere in his apologies.

John spent many years fighting his illness but always, always kept a positive attitude and continued to look for alternative methods to treat AIDS and all the other assorted ailments that go along with it. He thought it very important to advocate for ones own healthcare. He used to tell me that you couldn't always trust in your doctor to keep you informed of all the new and improved potions and pills because some of them simply did not know or care to know. Everyone must put a hand into their own wellness if they had any intentions of fighting back against their diseases. John was fortunate enough to have a very dedicated doctor and he always told John the truth in regards to his diagnosis.

I thought that I would continue to beat fate and be lucky enough to have John around for many years to come. That was not the case, and it all happened very quickly even though I had more than 13 years to prepare for it. You can never really prepare yourself for the death of a loved one with a terminal illness. You just have to deal with their death one day at a time, much the same way they did in living with their illness.

For many years I was in total denial and just refused to believe that he would die before he became an old man. But the reality is, anyone that has a terminal illness is going to die before you are and you better just get used to it. No matter how much you cry or try to ignore the big picture it is still there. So you have to be kind, be nurturing, loving, patient, supportive and most of all enjoy every minute you can with your loved ones, sick or healthy. You won't get another chance.

I hope that the people that read this book, (with or without a terminal illness), will find something in it that they can relate to or just remember a few of the words and thoughts; and that they will feel like John has somehow touched them too and given them a little comfort, a little truth, a little humor. I will never stop missing you John.

Printed in the United States
18269LVS00001B/97-99